Imagine There's No Beatles

An experiment in investigative speculative journalism

By Charlie Bermant

Copyright 2013 by Charlie Bermant

Copy editing: Angeline Higgins

THIS PAGE LEFT BLANK BY ACCIDENT

Forward!

Changing a past event is a popular conversational topic, how our lives would differ if we had or hadn't passed through a particular sliding door. Everyone's life is subject to such examination, but the stakes are raised when the person in question had a significant historical impact. What would have happened, you wonder, if Kennedy had lived longer or Hitler had died earlier?

The Beatles were world famous for six years before they dissolved and turned into legend. As their legacy grew fans scoured the rubble for new information. Even though their music was an incredible gift to the world many people felt cheated that it ended so soon.

Many have wished for more, creating fantasies about a reunion tour or album. But what if there were less? And what if there was enough to whet your appetite, to have it suddenly snatched away?

This story began as the first chapter of a speculative novel model where The Beatles were killed at the height of their fame only to rise again. The concept was flawed and never grew past this first chapter. Every writer has dozens of unwritten novels and this was destined for addition to my own slush pile.

Except technology changed book publishing. Not only can aspiring authors skip the painful publication dance, they can write anything regardless of length or content and publish it themselves. Getting people to read it is the hard part, but often it is enough of a reward to just publish the thing and get it our of the drawer.

Once upon a time not too long ago a 24-page satirical piece would remain unread forever as the author struggled for years to finish the other chapters. In extreme cases, it could be published after an author's death and gain them a fair amount of posthumous fame and fortune (although the marketing process is even more difficult after you're dead).

The bad news is that any random yahoo with a word processor and a half-baked idea can write and publish a book, so you have to hack through a lot of weeds to find an edible plant.

The good news is that the aforementioned yahoo can write to their own length rather than one dictated by a publisher and an English teacher. We don't have to draw out an idea just for its own sake. Additionally, the ever-diminishing average attention gives a short book a fighting chance,

Time travel and alternate universes have fascinated us for generations, both in literature and the living room. But if mankind really finds a way to unravel time's fabric it will be the end of the world as we know it. In the meantime it doesn't hurt to create some of these scenarios, just because we can.

Charlie Bermant
Port Townsend, WA
March 2013

POP GROUP KILLED IN EXPLOSION

MANILA, PHILIPPINES (REUTERS) JULY 4, 1966— All four members of the Beatles, an internationally famous pop combo with a string of hit records extending over three years, were killed when the boat on which they were staying exploded.

The group included guitarists John Lennon, 25, George Harrison, 23, Paul McCartney, 24, and 25-year-old Ringo Starr, a drummer.

The incident occurred in the late afternoon, after the band had played two concerts at Rezal Memorial Football Stadium, to a combined crowd of 80,000 people.

According to Malcolm Evans, the group's 31-year-old road manager, the band had been invited to meet Filipino First Lady Imelda Marcos at a pre-concert reception, but had declined. This alleged message did not reach the palace, resulting in Mrs. Marcos feeling slighted. She allegedly then dismissed The Beatles' security detail.

The band took refuge on a boat owned by a sympathetic fan and were attempting to secure a ride to the airport when the explosion occurred,

As the incident is under investigation relations have chilled considerably between Great Britain and the Philippines. Elsewhere there has occurred a tremendous outpouring of emotion similar to the response to United States President John F. Kennedy's assassination nearly three years ago.

"Many parents have thought of the Beatles as frivolous and

annoying," said Emma Reichert, a spokeswoman for the Bureau of Health in London. "But a lot if kids are taking this loss very personally, and several girls have tried to take their own lives."

"Thankfully none have succeeded but we are asking parents to watch their teenagers carefully for radical mood changes, especially girls who seem obsessed with the Beatles."

As news of the incident has traveled around the world fans have held large, loud public memorials.

Some Beatles fans do not accept the news and believe the group will re-emerge with another album and tour.

"I can't believe they are really gone," said Hillary Rodham, a fan from Chicago who was on holiday in London. "I know they are still alive and will wash up on a beach somewhere."

This is not possible, as the bodies of all four Beatles were identified by their manager, Brian Epstein.

In their four years of fame the quartet from Liverpool had 14 number one singles and released six albums in the United Kingdom.

A final album completed before the tour began was scheduled for release in August but has now been postponed indefinitely.

Final Beatles Album Poised for Release

ASSOCIATED PRESS

LOS ANGELES—The final album by the British pop group the Beatles will be released next month, the last recordings made before the singing group was killed in an explosion on July 4 of last year.
Since the incident, Capitol Records has released two albums, each featuring 11 of the band's best known and most popular songs, assembled from their four-year recording career. Both albums topped the music sales lists for the 1966 holiday season, and fell out of the top ten lists only last week.
The two albums frustrated many Beatles fans, since the label has repeatedly postponed the release of the album the band had completed at the time of its demise. This situation was exacerbated by the fact that the group's most recent album at that time, "Yesterday and Today," was itself a collection of previously released songs and those intended for its upcoming album.
Due to what was described as "emotional stress" Beatles' manager Brian Epstein was not involved in the preparation of the two greatest hits albums.
The new album is a more careful package than the two hastily assembled greatest hits albums, as Epstein supervised its release. He considered several lavish designs and presentations before settling on a simple format, a plain white cover with the lowercase words "the beatles" embossed on front of the album.
Even with this simplicity the album is one of the most expensive to produce in history, since the jackets are made with thick paper that simulates a linen finish.
There are two other Beatles albums prepared, taped live during various stages of their short career. Their release is uncertain, depending on how well the 'the beatles' does on the pop charts.
"It took me a long time to prepare this album and I apologize to the fans who were anxiously awaiting its release," Epstein said in a prepared statement.
"But I think the new album is what the boys would have wanted." **January 20, 1967**

Actor's Remarks Prompt Film Boycott, Actress Quits
Beatty apologizes to church, Kennedy family

Dunaway bails, Beatty flails: A movie that might not ever be made.

Variety, March 27, 1967

NEW YORK—Reaction to an admittedly "flip" comment by actor Warren Beatty on the Tonight Show last week threw the funding for his most recent film into jeopardy when financial support was withdrawn.
The actor is now looking for alternatives to finance the film, ' Bonnie and Clyde," which is based on the real-life exploits of Roaring 20s era gangsters Bonnie Parker and Clyde Barrow.
Beatty's remarks shocked many in Hollywood, with one prominent producer saying, "I really wonder what-or if- Warren was thinking."
"The Beatles' deaths hit a lot of people I know very hard," Beatty said on the show. "And for them, they felt a larger loss after that happened than after the assassination of President Kennedy."
After Beatty's remarks his co-star, Faye Dunaway, left the project to appear as the female lead in Roman Polanski's "Rosemary's Baby."
Beatty reacted to Dunaway's action with the announcement that he hired Carly Simon, a 21-year-old actress with no film experience to play Bonnie.
Beatty called a press conference on Thursday that was attended by about 40 reporters, where he explained that the remarks were "taken out of context."
According to Beatty his segment was running long, cutting into a scheduled appearance by comedian Buddy Hackett, who then refused to appear on the show. Beatty and host Johnny Carson were forced to improvise, and Carson asked about the Beatles to fill time.
Beatty said that the show ended in the middle of his answer to Carson, and that the context was not heard over the orchestra, "I did say that kids felt more about the Beatles than President

Kennedy," he said. "But I added how that was really misguided because Kennedy will go down in history as one of our greatest presidents, and the Beatles will most likely be forgotten in a year or two."

Beatty acknowledged that his original comment "was a bit too flip."

Beatty's intention was to defuse criticism of his earlier remarks, but he made it worse with his clarifying statement. After about twenty minutes Beatty's manager ended the press conference. But Beatty "had one more thing" to say, quoting one of the last interviews given by the late John Lennon in which he said the Beatles "were more popular than Jesus."

"John Lennon knew about the power of fame and how it skews public perception," Beatty said. "His statement about how the band had become more popular than Jesus was not a boast but a lament."

A few hours after the press conference Beatty's agent announced the actor has apologized to the Kennedy family for his original statement, and is reportedly preparing an additional apology to Catholic leaders.

Dear Cher
...and Sonny

SONNY AND I are in the pages of 16, here to answer your questions and help you to solve the problems of everyday life. We really care about you, our fans, so if you don't see your question included here know that we carefully select a cross-section of your letters to reflect your most important problems. If we don't answer your question please come back next month, because the problems and the advice right here in 16 includes some very valuable advice.

Dear Cher,
I am upset about The Beatles and am sad that they had to die, but the truth is I never really liked their music all that much. I pretended to because people treated me strangely when I said that I liked the Beach Boys way better. Now I can't say anything at all, because if you say the Beatles weren't the best thing no one will ask you to any parties. It's getting harder to lie. What would you do?

Pretending
West Hurley, NY

Dear Pretending,
When someone dies people say nice things about them and forget about what they didn't like, and it is rude to say bad things about someone if they aren't there to respond. This really isn't about what you like, it's more about the ability to show respect. If your friend's grandmother died and you didn't like her you would never tell your friend because it wouldn't do any good. So if you want to say something bad about the Beatles pretend they are your friend's grandmother, and talk about something else. You can't help your feelings, but you shouldn't feel there is anything wrong with you if you don't like what everyone else likes. Differences are what make us interesting. But it also is a good thing to keep an open mind. Maybe in a few months when school is out you should

listen to the Beatles again. You may decide that you really like them, and that your previous opinion was based on a desire to be different from anybody else.

Dear Sonny;
Last year the girl I really liked wouldn't go with me because she said she was going to marry George Harrison, so I stopped asking. This year I asked again because the marriage won't happen now obviously. She says she is still in "mourning" and won't give up her vow to George at least until he's been gone a year. This is bad news for me, because there is a dance at the end of school where I want to take her. I'm not sure what to do, I want to keep asking but lately I wonder whether if she just doesn't like me and is using George as an excuse. What do you think?
Kenny
Amherst, MA

Dear Kenny,
Girls don't always know what they want from one minute to the next, but it looks like this one's mind is made up if she's turned you down for a whole year. But if you feel like she is the one for you don't give up just yet. She may be a little scared that she would lose you in the same way that she lost George. I don't know what you look like, but it may break the ice if you can try to look something like George in little ways. Maybe get the same kind of haircut. If you can't look like him maybe you can capture his personality and act like him a little bit. Acting can be hard but you won't have to do it forever. Once she gets to like you and go out a few times you can stop pretending and be yourself.

Dear Cher and Sonny,
I really like 16 and your column is cool, but I'm really sick of hearing about the Beatles all the time. There are more stories about them now than when they were alive, and there is no way that we can ever meet them or go out with them. That may have been unlikely back then, but at least there was a chance. So I wish you would stop writing about the Beatles and talk about people with other problems, like mine. All of my friends have boyfriends but I don't. But I don't want one. A boy took me out and kissed me but I didn't feel anything. I would rather be in the next room talking to his sister than

kissing him. Is this normal?
Betsy
Silverton, OR

Dear Betsy.
You are maybe a bit more particular than normal but that doesn't have to be a bad thing. You also could be more of a mental than a physical person and want to have a good conversation with someone before you kiss him. This is normal because girls often grow up faster than boys so you may be more at ease talking to the boy's sister even if she is younger than he is. If his sister is really interesting you may want to keep that friendship, because when her brother finally grows up and you like him better he will be comfortable around you.

That's it for now. If you have a problem--whether it has anything to do with the Beatles or not--write us at the address below and we will try to help you.
Our address is:

DEAR CHER (or)
DEAR SONNY
16 Magazine
745 Fifth Avenue
New York, N.Y. 10022

CRAWDADDY!/The Rock Magazine
What the Boys Would Have Wanted?

By Nels Paulsen

In order to appreciate the mixed masterpiece that is the Beatles' final album we have to first understand what it is not, then what it could have possibly become.
While the songs on the album were already recorded when an as-yet-unexplained boat explosion took their lives, the group was absent when the album was prepared for release. So while this is their own music and was not altered after their deaths, the group had nothing to do with the song order, album cover, album title or promotion. All of these responsibilities were assumed by people who didn't necessarily have the group's best interests or their legacy in mind.
We will never know for certain how this music would have appeared if the band had lived, only that it would have emerged in the summertime, when its optimistic sounds would have been synchronized with the season. As they arrive in the dead of winter, this cold mood has exaggerated the sense of sadness when you listen to what you know will be their last album for the first time.
It does not have all the songs that the Beatles had recorded when they did not know it would be their last. Missing is "Here, There and Everywhere," last summer's melancholy hit record which was plucked from the finished tracks and released as a single (backed by the equally melodic and just a little cheerier "If I Needed Someone" from "Yesterday and Today").
While many of the songs explore and expand the experiments taken on "Rubber Soul" and "Yesterday and Today," the

session's most experimental track is also missing. Untitled, it reportedly features a repetitive drone over which Lennon chants obscure lyrics about turning on, tuning in and dropping off the face of the earth. Ringo's drumming is, as always, steadfast and inspired.

There are those who swear that it does not exist, because if it did and really was so extraordinary then Capitol would have no other choice but to include it on the album.

But it does exist, and is already available in many New York record stores- although sold under the counter in a plain white sleeve and with no text on the label.

Beatles fans waiting for the logical follow-up to "Rubber Soul," which is now an inconceivable 14 months old, will be disappointed by this lower-case effort. But it could have been much different and a whole lot worse.

The two posthumous Beatles albums have been hit repackages, one featuring singles and the most popular album tracks from 1962 to 1964 and another from 1965 and 1966. Both feature the same cover picture, you can only tell the difference between the two because one has a red border and the other is blue.

Were they alive, one thinks the Beatles would never have agreed to such a cheap device.

At the time of the accident they were the one remaining British band of significance to resist the impulse to release "greatest hits" albums. By comparison, Herman's Hermits (which has enjoyed a bump in popularity due perhaps to fans craving anything that sounds remotely like the Beatles) has two such records.

This album is not, as Brian Epstein said, "what the boys would have wanted." Were they alive, the Beatles would not have put out an album with only two songs performed by John Lennon. And if there were only two Lennon songs, one would not have been a stray B-side to a year-old single.

"Rain" is still pretty good, and its presence here will placate those who want all of the Beatles songs to be on an album whether they fit or not. And the other Lennon song, "I Know What it's Like to Be Dead," kicks off the album, and sets the mood.

So even if there are only two Lennon songs here John still casts the biggest shadow. It would have been different if this shortage had occurred when they were alive, and he would have written a few more tunes to balance things out.

Or it would have been different if Capitol Records hadn't pulled three unfinished Lennon songs. "I'm Only Sleeping," "And Your Bird Can Sing" and "Dr. Robert," for "Yesterday and Today." (The three songs are included on the British version of the new album, making it as much Lennon's as McCartney's.)

Even so, you don't notice the Lennon deficit right away, since the first four songs feature John, Paul, George and Ringo in sequence. "I Know What it's Like to Be Dead" is followed by "Good Day Sunshine," "I Want to Tell You" and "Yellow Submarine. John, Paul, George and Ringo. The album's first real statement is that the band, despite all else, was a demonstration of how the band's whole exceeded its four parts.

The first side finishes with a pair of McCartney songs, very different from each other. "Got to Get You Into My Life" is horn-driven pop with a great hook, the kind of stuff the Beatles could do in their sleep but amazes every time. "I'm Down" is a great song, but again you wonder why it's here. It's even older than "Rain" and was the b-side of "Help" back in Summer 1965.

But "I'm Down" pays tribute to the songs by Little Richard and Chuck Berry that filled out their early albums before they learned to write all their old songs. For their last album it makes sense to include something that acknowledges their roots.

Side two begins with another retread, "Paperback Writer," followed by Harrison's "Taxman" and McCartney's "Eleanor Rigby." This song was released for the Christmas season as a McCartney solo single, for that reason it sticks out here. "For No One," another soft Paul song, is next.

"Rain" follows and then a surprise. Even if Lennon and McCartney were the group's leaders Harrison's "Make Love All Day Long" has the last word. "Love me while you can," he intones over the drone of several sitars. "Before I'm a dead old man." Harrison played the sitar on "Norwegian Wood" on "Rubber Soul," as if it were an atonal acoustic guitar. Here it becomes a wall of subcontinent sound, grim and hypnotic.

And what would they have done, had they lived? Recording artists of today are bursting with ideas. Some, like Brian Wilson's brilliant sunny "Smile" was doubly liberating: Wilson declared independence from the Beach Boy straightjacket and did this one all on his own.

Others, like the Dave Clark Five's "John Barleycorn's Roaming Pub Crawl Orchestra," are well-intentioned but the themes fall short after you've heard the records a few times. One would think the Beatles would have given us a conceptual experience that improved with repeated listens.

The Beatles would have been at the forefront of this renaissance, but the revolution has gone on without them. Is this album what "the boys" would have wanted? Not likely. But it's good enough that we will probably still be listening to it, and all the Beatles had done in their short lives, and it won't be a surprise if we are still listening to this music when we grow into our 30s. Which is, unfortunately, something the Beatles never got the chance to do.

THE PLAYBOY INTERVIEW:
Brian Epstein

The loss of the Beatles last year was a devastating blow to the world of popular music, from which it may not recover for some time.
Beatles manager Brian Epstein, however, is well on the way to his own recovery. Last summer, after the Beatles died in an explosion, Epstein was completely traumatized and lost control of the band's first two posthumous projects.
Even as the rest of the world mourned the Beatles, Epstein's grief was deeply personal. He did not create the group, nor did he "discover" them in a literal sense. Instead, he sensed their potential to become a phenomenon as soon as he saw them perform in Liverpool.
During the subsequent years the Beatles evolved from a very promising young band to one that changed the world. Then they were gone.
Epstein, who was in the middle of the group's maelstrom from the beginning, went into what he described as "immediate shock" after hearing the news.
Today much has changed. He has not recovered from the loss of his protegees, and his frequent, polite smiles seem quite mournful. He fidgets quite a bit and often changes the subject in the middle of a sentence.
He has, however, jettisoned several bad habits such as smoking and drinking. In an unguarded moment he admitted

using amphetamines, but there is no doubt that he has cleaned up and is healthier than he's ever been.
Adding to this is his new sense of peace brought about by his admission here in these pages that some will find startling.

PLAYBOY: What's your announcement?

EPSTEIN: Some might not find this a surprise, but I am homosexual.

PLAYBOY: Why are you telling us this, and why now?

EPSTEIN: After what happened last summer I was forced to look at myself and what I could possibly do next, keeping in mind that I lost my entire world just months ago. I decided that I couldn't continue to hide this fact from other people. As for why here, your magazine reaches an enlightened audience, at least when it comes to sexual matters, so I know you aren't going to take things out of context. That will come later, as your daily press here will focus on the scandalous bits and play up the most sordid aspects.

PLAYBOY: So this changes your life.

EPSTEIN: It is only a small part of what I am, but was actually much bigger when I was trying to hide it. Now that I have admitted it, "out of the closet" as is the new popular term, I don't feel threatened byits exposure.

PLAYBOY: People threatened you?

EPSTEIN: There was always a fear…while the Beatles were on top everything was moving so fast, and we often reacted to the situations in ways that we wouldn't have when if we had time to think.

PLAYBOY: Which means?

EPSTEIN: You can't imagine the attention, how the world paid attention to everything the Beatles did. They were followed everywhere and the girls would just start screaming. You see it on the television, or in magazines, but being there was quite different. So The Beatles reacted under stress, and I had to deal with the consequences. Right before we left on the last tour we learned that an interview John had given saying the Beatles were more popular than Jesus was going to be published in America, during the tour. I knew I was going to have to control the damage and I wasn't looking forward to that.

PLAYBOY: I don't see the connection between.....

EPSTEIN: There isn't one, really, except I had to manage the Beatles and watch my back at the same time, A double life, as it were, so when I woke up from my long sleep I knew there was a lot of work to be done, and undone because the last two albums shouldn't have come out. I needed to set things straight with the new record, and thought it would be easier if I didn't have to lie along the way.
The biggest argument against me telling the truth before, not that it was really discussed, was that if people knew that I was homosexual it would have lost fans for the Beatles. Looking back, it wouldn't have been a disaster if they had fewer fans, fewer people who were trying to tear them apart.

PLAYBOY: Or maybe it would have been worse.

EPSTEIN: Truth is, it was never discussed. When I...do you want to talk about the Beatles at all?

PLAYBOY: I thought we were.

EPSTEIN: (fidgets)

PLAYBOY: So The Beatles left a tremendous void in music, even though there are still a lot of people creating some marvelous stuff. Will that void ever be filled?

EPSTEIN: Eventually, but not in the same way. We can't force it, as I've found.

PLAYBOY: In what respect?

EPSTEIN: One of the groups that I was working with, three brothers from the Isle of Man called the BeeGees, sounded very much like the Beatles to me, so I asked them to record some of the unrecorded songs the Beatles had written, or partially written, for the BeeGees to record, But they refused. The oldest one is just 20, but he had a real mind of his own, and went against me directly, saying "I'm sorry Mr. Epstein but we have our own songs that we want to record. After we do them if you don't like them we'll do it your way."

This kid-Barry was arguing with me about a particular song, saying that I wanted it to sound too much like the Beatles. I was put off at first but then I remembered when I first met the Beatles and they were the same way. So I let Barry and his brothers follow their instincts, and their first album is remarkable, Some of it does sound like the Beatles quite a bit. I don't think you can avoid that right now, consciously or not every group sounds like the Beatles.

PLAYBOY: And you are managing them?

EPSTEIN: Not completely. The most I did was find them some people to fill out their sound. The three brothers sing, play guitar and bass respectively, I found them a guitarist and a drummer. The guitar player is a remarkable 16-year-old named Peter Frampton, while I can't say who the drummer is yet. I was involved with every step of the Beatles lives, something they were beginning to resent, I think. So I've decided to let other people do some of the work, "delegate," if you will. The BeeGees will be handled by my associate Robert Stigwood, and he'll check in with me regularly. I've also signed an American guitarist named Jimmy Hendrix, who is being managed by Chas Chandler, whom I knew when he was in the Animals.

The Beatles took all of my attention, so in my second act I'm going to let others handle all the details, and help out from behind the scenes. There is no reason that I have to do everything anymore. I don't have the energy, and I don't want to be as personally involved.

This may sound crass, but if I am not so invested in those I manage, my clients, then I won't be as hurt when they go away.

PLAYBOY: But none of these groups can take the Beatles' place.

EPSTEIN: Well, no, but there is a lot of creativity and I can help it come to pass. The BeeGees and Jimmy Hendrix are only two examples. Additionally, there are a several "second generation" musicians who were in good bands and are finding new combinations. Jeff Beck, for one, is a wonderful guitar player who never really found his niche in the Yardbirds, and I've paired him with Eric Burdon, who sang for the Animals. They clicked right away in rehearsals and have recorded a few songs but have yet to find the right drummer and bass player.

PLAYBOY: So you're the matchmaker?

EPSTEIN: The Beatles succeeded because they were four strong personalities that blended into a whole. If I can help a "John" find his "Paul" it will make it worthwhile. Creative people don't always make the wisest choices. So by pairing up Jeff and Eric, who would never choose each other on their own, I am using my instincts to help them make great music.

PLAYBOY: But music isn't just business.

EPSTEIN: No, of course not. Jeff and Eric, they wouldn't argue with me for saying this, are both tremendously egotistical. They each want to be the center of attention. So having a group with two centers I think will be very exciting.

PLAYBOY: Like the Beatles.

EPSTEIN: Not really, The Beatles actually had four centers,. People perceived John and Paul as the leaders, but their success came from the blend of all of them. They are all gone now, so we'll never know, but if one of them left the band they could not have carried on. The Beatles had to end all at once.

CONTINUED ON PAGE 232

STROLLING CLONE, Nov. 12, 1967

BYRDS DROPPING

Left to Right: David Crosby, Brian Wilson, Roger McGuinn

BY YAHN WIENER

David Crosby is in a very good mood. After a rocky year when the Byrds were fractured by internal dissent he has emerged victorious and is now leading the group into what may be its most fertile and creative period.
"This is what's gonna happen," he said, biting into a huge Granny Smith. "We'll make an album with just the four of us (himself, Chris Hillman, Mike Clarke and newly added guitarist Stephen Stills) and then invite some other people in to jam." Among those he mentions are Jefferson Airplane's Paul Kantner, Bob Dylan and Eric Clapton although none of them have been contacted about the opportunity.
 Crosby is also excited about a lesser known singer, whom he is attempting to lure away from The Hollies.
 "There is a guy that no one's heard over here named Allan Clarke," Crosby said. "He's great at harmony and when he sings with Steve and me it goes into a whole other thing. I'd like to see him in the Byrds."
Crosby picks up his guitar and plays a newly written but untitled song, about King Arthur's Court called "Guinevere Had Green Eyes Like Yours." He stops singing after two verses and starts talking about the Beatles. "It was hard for everyone when that happened but it was harder for us," he said. "People were looking to us for answers, to pick up where the Beatles left off. We started playing a few Beatles songs onstage just out of respect, but pretty soon that's all some people wanted to hear. "And some other people," he said with a visible sneer, "wanted to give it to them."

Crosby is referring to Roger McGuinn, once a key part of the Byrds, all afternoon but this is the first time he's mentioned his former friend by name.

"McGuinn took it really hard," he said. "We all did, but he lost his way. First thing he wanted to do a few Beatles songs onstage and we did that. 'If I Needed Someone' sounded really good.

"Except he wanted to put it out as a single, and follow it up with a whole album of their songs. I pushed back."

The straw that broke the sparrows' backs was McGuinn's surprise onstage appearance playing guitar in a makeshift band assembled by Brian Wilson to perform at last summer's Monterey Pop Festival.

"I didn't care that he was playing with Brian, man," Crosby said. "It was the sneaking around, and the fact that we didn't know he was playing until he was already up there."

Crosby's full control of the Byrds will become clear this month when their new album, "Notorious,' hits the streets. The album was mostly complete when McGuinn was fired, and Crosby went into the studio and replaced all of McGuinn's vocals with his own.

The capper is the cover, which shows the outside of a stable with a band member in each stall—except McGuinn's stall is occupied by a Clydesdales' rear end. "Jimmy acted like a horse's ass," Crosby said. "And right now we don't feel like forgiving him."

But McGuinn is one happy horse's ass. He may have lost a gig in one of the scene's brightest bands, but playing with Brian Wilson is a pretty fair consolation prize.

He put a lot of effort into the Byrds, but after the Beatles' demise it wasn't fun anymore.

Playing his own songs wasn't as rewarding as something by Lennon and McCartney. And Harrison, too. The McGuinn-led Byrds rendition of "If I Needed Someone" sounded better than the original, to some ears.

"Byrds songs were descended from Beach Boys songs as much as Beatles songs," he said about his old band. "We listened to a lot of other people's music, but recorded what we heard in our own heads." With the Beatles gone, McGuinn felt the balance between the Byrds and the Beach Boys was way off kilter. Playing with Brian Wilson seemed to be an obvious solution. He said he knew Crosby would be upset but chose to "ask for forgiveness rather than permission," but what began as an adventure soon turned difficult. "The thing about Brian is that he needs to rehearse everything a hundred times," McGuinn said. "There were some incredible new songs but very precise. It became hard for me to keep up two faces and the whole thing almost came crashing down when I accidentally played part of "Good Vibrations" on one of David's songs."

While McGuinn's presence onstage with Wilson visibly annoyed Crosby the resulting music was extraordinary enough to offset the fact that McGuinn knew he was going to get a talking to. And while Crosby is eager to call McGuinn names this does not go both ways. When asked whether Crosby was too controlling McGuinn answers "David is doing his thing, and I'm doing mine."

When we ask about Crosby again we get nothing but a silent glare. But the next time Brian Wilson's name comes up McGuinn picks up the phone. "Let's go see him now," he said. "I'll make sure he's at home."

Wilson is out playing tennis, so he meets us at his house an hour later, dripping with sweat. He opens the door himself seconds after we ring the bell. He has a glass of milk in each hand passing them to us one at a time, then retreats to the kitchen from where he retrieves his own glass. "I'm glad Roger brought you over," Wilson said without preamble. "I want you to hear some new songs."

He plays six, all with a definable Beach Boys/Brian Wilson sound, but enhanced with chiming twelve-string guitar and harmonies not as precise as those on the final Beach Boys' album, "Pet Sounds."

The first song on the tape is "Wild Honey," a rocker shouted by Carl Wilson over a throbbing Theremin and McGuinn's soaring guitar. His solo begins where his noodling on "Eight Miles High" left off, racing the Theremin to the end of the instrumental break before Carl comes in with the final verse. "Change is Now," a McGuinn song, was recorded by the Byrds but left off their last album. The middle is lifted with a rich four-part harmony, with McGuinn and the three Wilson brothers. Here, you realize that the vocal authenticity comes from Dennis Wilson, whose voice is not as refined as Brian and Carl.

Four other songs-"Friends,' "Let the Wind Blow," "Here

Comes the Night" and "Goin' Back" finish the tape. The final song is written by Goffin-King, the same team that wrote highbrow stuff like "Do the Locomotion." But this is a beautiful piece, ironically the one where McGuinn and the three Wilsons emerge as equals.

Wilson lets the last note fade and switches off the tape.

"I could never have cut those songs with the Beach Boys," he said. "Bless them, but they didn't understand what I wanted to do and I didn't want to explain it to them. Al (Jardine) and Mike (Love) hated "Pet Sounds" and I refused to go through all that again with "Smile." And I've gone in a different direction since then."

There would be no Beach Boys without Wilson, and his breaking up the band could have doomed Love and Jardine to obscurity. Wilson, generously, has allowed the two-along with Wilson touring replacement Bruce Johnston-to continue performing as the Beach Boys.

People attending recent Beach Boys have expressed disappointment there are no Wilson brothers onstage. Brian actually stopped touring in 1964, but Carl was an acceptable substitute, and there was always Denny on the drums.

The new-model Beach Boys sound authentic enough- after all, Brian rehearsed them-but they lack authenticity. Even so, they are pretty exciting, speeding up the songs to fit about thirty into an hour's time, then adding a few encores. The adrenalin, at least for this tour, comes from a substitute drummer, 21-year-old Keith Moon, who recently left the remarkable but virtually unknown in America band called the Who.

"Keith came backstage during the last British tour and offered to step in if they ever needed a drummer," Brian said. "It bothered Denny at the time, but made him feel less guilty when he wanted to quit. He remembered the English kid and gave him a call. Luckily enough, he has the year free until his next project."

Moon will continue drumming for the Beach Boys until March, when he is due to join a new group with Jeff Beck and Eric Burdon. "We'll find Mike and Al a new drummer then," Brian said. "It doesn't really matter who's playing these songs, really."

Brian's agreement with the Beach Boys doesn't allow them to record new music but he doesn't think that'll be a problem.

"I know those guys," he said. "They'll be happy if they can play those same songs, over and over, forever."

Monkees Shine, NBC Squints

NBC has officially canceled 'The Monkees" after the cast and crew conspired to change a previously rehearsed live segment to concoct what network executives called a "subversive" message.
A statement released by producer Donnie Kirschner said "the Monkees played a good natured prank they felt was in keeping with their happy go lucky image. Unfortunately, they violated standards of good taste."
A network source said on Tuesday that the decision to cancel could have gone either way "but the group did not apologize for their actions, and we can't have actors using the airwaves to broadcast their personal opinions."
The script called for all four members, one at a time, to sit down on a shoeshine platform, striking up a casual, holiday-based conversation with the bootblack who was seen from the rear. At the end of the sketch the four were directed to stand up and say "Merry Christmas!" and hug the shoeshine man.
In the script the face of the shoeshine man was not visible, although it was obvious that he was a Negro. On the air, the four group members gave holiday greetings directed toward four holidays: Christmas, Hanukah, Ramadan and a made-up holiday called "Festivus" before the bootblack turned around, raised his fist and spoke out for "holiday power to all people."
The actor playing the bootleg bootblack was later identified as Jesse Jackson, 25, a sometime associate of Dr. Martin Luther King.
The group and its producer meant this as a message in support of racial equality, and had to change the script several times in order to satisfy the network's censors, who felt it would alienate areas where race relations were fragile. Telephone switchboards were immediately jammed, and the show was not broadcast on the West Coast.
As news of the cancellation spread Monkees fans in both New York and Burbank, CA staged protests at network headquarters.
The show was one of 1967's most popular new series, although it had an uncertain start. It was originally intended to begin airing in September 1966, translating the zaniness of the Beatles two movies into a comedy format. Four actor-

musicians were cast in the series, but it was postponed after the Beatles were killed in a riot on July 4, 1966. The series was then recast and rewritten to be "a little more serious and political" for audiences who
were still in shock after the loss of the Beatles. Former child star Micky Dolenz was the only member of the original cast who was retained. The three new members were Steve Martin, 21, a comedy writer and banjo player, California songwriter Harry Nilsson, 25, and Todd Rundgren, a 19-year-old guitar prodigy from Philadelphia.

The first few episodes of the Monkees' TV show were uneven and, as many critics said, unfunny. It was threatened with cancellation after just a few episodes but audience numbers increased after a series of topical episodes ended the first season. "We had such a small audience that the network figured they'd let us do what we wanted," Martin said in an interview at the beginning of the 1967 fall season for TV Guide. "It backfired for them, because more people started watching." Martin didn't comment about NBC's decision, and according to his manager has many roles to choose from.

Not if NBC has any say. Network president Steve Flower said last week "these guys are all finished in show business. You will never hear the names Micky Dolenz, Todd Rundgren, Harry Nilsson, Steve Martin or Jesse Jackson again."

DECEMBER 19, 1967

Washington Merry Go Round
JOHNSON: Concerns About King's Safety

By Drew Pearson

President Lyndon Johnson doesn't watch a lot of television, especially those programs geared toward frivolous entertainment, but by chance happened to see a portion of the comedy show, "The Monkees," just before Christmas.
My source tells me the president was relaxing after a long day and the television was on in the background when a Christmas skit that included a young Negro leader in a raised salute was broadcast. That particular skit caused a lot of controversy and adverse reaction, since the actors were not following the script.
It resulted in the cancellation of the show and the chastising of the leader, Jesse Jackson, by his boss, Rev. Martin Luther King. King, it was reported, was told by his advisers to distance himself from Jackson's protest action, and by all accounts is following that advice.
But Johnson had quite a different reaction. My source told me he sat silently for about twenty minutes and picked up the phone, calling King directly and expressing concern about his safety. My source was not in a position to write down Johnson's exact words, but later reconstructed them as "Martin, I am worried that someone will see this broadcast, get a crazy idea and come after you."

The president then attempted to get King to meet with law enforcement officials to provide extra protection, a suggestion that prompted an immediate negative reaction. But Johnson, turning on all his persuasive powers, brought up the name of a King associate who, it turns out, is a government agent feeding selected information back to the Justice Department. Johnson said that it was possible for agents to blend in with the King entourage and provide protection without disrupting King's mission.

This includes a "Poor People's Campaign" where King intends to stage a massive demonstration in Washington this spring. This demonstration could be even bigger than the March on Washington for Jobs and Freedom, which drew 200,000 people to Washington on August 26, 1963.

King doesn't trust law enforcement, and he admires-but does not actually trust-the president. Whether or not Johnson can persuade King to accept help with security, the warning has already sounded. People in King's camp are no more aware of the potential threat. Johnson doesn't completely trust King, but realizes the two leaders can help each other to achieve mutual goals.

Johnson is gearing up for a re-election campaign, and knows that support from King will be essential if he is to defeat either of the Republican favorites, Nelson Rockefeller or Richard Nixon. He also needs some positive news, to offset the anti-Vietnam War rumblings that are beginning to shake the country.

I predict that the two leaders will come to an agreement. King will take Johnson's suggestions to heart, and the march will proceed with the president's tacit cooperation. This will give Johnson a political advantage.

This time next year, as Johnson is sworn in for his final term, the two will be working together in favor of King's dream.

January 7, 1968

The End of an Era: Nasty Bee Gees split leaves new album in tatters

Melody Maker, January 12 1969

The BeeGees are no more.
While it may not have been as dramatic as the accident that took the lives of the Beatles, it is the second time in less than three years the biggest pop group in the world has crashed and burned.
Right after the first of the year Robin Gibb, who with older brother Barry and twin Maurice provided the BeeGees core, sued his brothers and its managers, Brian Epstein and Robert Stigwood for the dissolution of the band and as the suit states, "distribution of all financial and physical assets."
Sources close to the band claim to have seen the split coming for several months. Their once happy-go-lucky attitude has been replaced by jealousy and tension, and efforts to keep up a brave face for the fans didn't always work.
The final fracture occurred when Stigwood decided to release Barry's "Lonely Days" as the A side of the new single, delegating Robin's "How Can You Mend A Broken Heart" to the flip. Upon learning this Robin left the studio and has not talked to his brothers since.
Ironically, the two-sided disc has become the band's biggest hit as well as 1968's best selling single worldwide.
It's a sad end for a band that went from talented unknowns to surrogate Beatles within a few months.
In 1966 Barry, Robin and Maurice Gibb were the biggest pop stars in Australia and were contemplating ways to broaden their audience when the Beatles were killed in an Manila boat explosion.
"When we first saw the Beatles we said 'that's what we want to do' but we weren't good enough yet," Barry told *Melody Maker* last year. "It took another two years to get up the nerve and we were all set to book steamship tickets when the Beatles

were killed. That threw us off kilter and we didn't sing or play for weeks until we got the call."

"The call" came from Stigwood, an Australian who had moved to England in 1954 and was then working as an independent promoter and producer. Stigwood flew the three brothers to London, who did four label auditions within two days of landing on British soil.

The band signed with Polydor in October 1966 and set out to record their first album, titled *Bee Gees First.* Kicking off with "To Love Somebody," the album brought immediate comparisons to the Beatles for its ability to blend a variety of styles and melodies. Stigwood also struck up a partnership with Epstein who was looking to recapture the Beatles' magic and made the BeeGees a priority.

First, released in February 1967, was followed by *Second* eight months later and *Third* in March 1968. Like the Beatles, the BeeGees made richly textured albums with few weak tracks and did not repeat themselves. After the pop oriented first album they shifted to a harder rock sound with the second album and again into a symphonic realm for the third.

It was when the band settled in to record their fourth album the facade cracked. Even as each album was full of hits and powerfully experimental music but much of *Third* was composed and recorded separately. It all came to a head when Barry and Robin each came up with the worthy songs that under almost any other circumstances would each be an automatic "A" side.

While no official statements have been made, a BeeGees sideman reports that Barry and Maurice are now wrestling the rough tapes from what was to be *Bee Gees Fourth* into a real album. That might not happen if Robin demands that his vocals be removed.

"Some of the tracks sound pretty good," said Peter Frampton, who joined the BeeGees during the *First* sessions. "But if Robin doesn't let us use his singing they're going to have to start from scratch. And I don't think that Barry and Maurice are up to doing it all over again."

Frampton use of "they" indicates that he is no longer with the band. After Robin walked out Stigwood called Frampton to his office to say the guitarist was "no longer needed."

For this reason Frampton is willing to share some inside information, confirming the rumor that Barry and Maurice have called in American producer Phil Spector to assemble the unfinished tapes into a cohesive album.

Frampton added that the differences aren't only musical, opining that Robin quit because he can't stand Barry's new wife.

"Robin really hates Yoko," Frampton said. "She's a pretty weird bird anyway, and the fact she is 13 years older than Barry made Robin really uncomfortable. Barry didn't care though, he really loves her and wants to be around her all the time."

That caused problems in a band where the members have known each other since birth and have played music together well before they graduated into long pants.

"They all have grown up a lot over the last few years and were starting to be a bit more independent," Frampton, himself only 18, said. "After being together all their lives they were turning into different people and it was starting to make e the music more interesting. But Barry brought Yoko to the studio and she started making suggestions and Robin freaked."

Cast of characters: John Lennon, Paul McCartney, George Harrison, Ringo Starr, Mal Evans, Imelda Marcos, Brian Epstein, Hillary Rodham, Warren Beatty, Faye Dunaway, Carly Simon, Sonny and Cher, Keith Moon, Jeff Beck, Eric Burdon, David Crosby, Brian Wilson, Roger McGuinn, Micky Dolenz, Todd Rundgren, Harry Nilsson, Steve Martin, Jesse Jackson, Drew Pearson, Lyndon Johnson, Martin Luther King, The BeeGees, Peter Frampton, and Yoko Ono.

Dinah DiNova

Charlie Bermant is the author of *A Serious Hobby*, a collection of interviews of some of pop music's brightest lights. He has worked as a political, technology and entertainment writer and is currently community journalist in the Puget Sound area. He can be contacted at **aserioushobby@gmail.com**

Made in the USA
San Bernardino, CA
01 April 2014